Be Positive, Think Positive, Feel Positive!

Surviving Primary School Vol. 2

By: Dr. Orly Katz

Illustrations: zofit shalom

ALL RIGHTS RESERVED. No part of this report may be reported in any form whatsoever, electronic, or mechanical, including photocopying, recording or by any informational storage or retrieval system without express written, dated and signed permission from the author.

DISCLAIMER AND/OR LEGAL NOTICES: the information presented in this report represents the views of the publisher as of the date of publication. The publisher reserves the rights to alter and update their opinions based on new conditions. This report is for informational purposes only. The author and the publisher do not accept any responsibilities for any liabilities resulting from the use of this information. While every attempt has been made to verify the information provided here, the author and the publisher cannot assume any responsibility for errors, inaccuracies or omissions. Any similarities with people or facts are unintentional.

About Dr. Orly Katz

Best seller author, Dr. Orly Katz, is an expert for youth empowerment and life skills, who hold a doctorate in Educational Leadership;

She is a sought after guest on TV and radio, and a national speaker and work shop facilitator for parents, educationalists and youth.

Orly is the founder of the "Simply Me" Center for: Leadership, Empowerment and Self Esteem.

Her two book series: Surviving Junior High, and Surviving Primary School, are recommended by the Ministry of Education, and are being taught in many schools as part of the curriculum in life skills lessons.

Orly lives in Haifa, with her Husband and three children.

Please don't hesitate to contact Orly at any time, at: www.SimplyMeModel.com

Table of Contents:

Introduction

The Key to the Power of Thought

A True Story- A Positive Attitude

The Rule for Perfection

The Rule for the Power of Thought

A True Story- Inferiority Complexes

The Rule for Inferiority Complexes

Questionnaire- Do you suffer from an inferiority complex?

A True Story- Birthday Tears

The Rule for Pessimists

The Rule for Optimists

Simply Me – Writing about Myself –Worksheets

Summary

Introduction

Dear Readers,

I want to congratulate you on your decision to take action and learn how to survive primary school by joining me in this, the second book of the series!

In each of the four books in the series we discover new keys which together unlock the secret of being 'Simply Me' and together teach you how to believe in yourself and gain self confidence and self esteem.

Anyone in primary school knows just how tough it is to:

- Think positive, especially when something has gone wrong and you are feeling awful...

- Like yourself even when your face is covered in zits, you've put on ten pounds and you have an inferiority complex...

- Believe in yourself even when you weren't invited to that special party ...

I've got great news for you; it really doesn't have to be like that...

Things don't have to be so hard. There are times that we all get upset and feel helpless, and there are other times when we feel on top of the world!

Growing up isn't easy. People suffered from the same things in the past that they suffer from now and will carry on suffering in the future. Our parents tried being cool, our grandparents flirted with each other once upon a time, Abraham Lincoln had pockmarked skin (which may be why he grew a beard!), Cleopatra had bad hair days and even President Barak Obama asked Michelle out for ice cream and got turned down the first time!

Whether it's today, in the 21st Century, or back in the Eighties, or the Sixties, or in the Renaissance, or even back in the days of the Stone Age growing up and being completely happy with who you are was hard, really, really hard.

Try imagining the next few scenes:

Growing up at the time of the Renaissance

I worked for days and days on the painting; I had been looking secretly through my window at the beautiful daughter of the cloth merchant from Florence, at Lisa. Lisa would appear in all of my dreams, sometimes looking mysterious, sometimes smiling...

I wanted to give her a present, a portrait, the portrait of her.

The day that I felt that the painting was finally perfect I strapped my finest belt round my waist, with my name -Leonardo- embroidered on it with finest gemstones.

I asked my two best friends to join me singing a serenade and playing on the lute. I spread the painting out beneath her window, and waited to see her delicate hand holding out an embroidered kerchief to me as a sign that she accepted the painting and my courtship.

And my Lisa, my beloved Lisa did stretch out her delicate hand – but oh-only to slam her window shut, draw the blind and bolt it closed.

I stayed with my painting that nobody wanted or took any notice of ...with my Mona Lisa...

Growing up in the sixties

The war in Vietnam had broken out, and I just wanted peace and quiet, and more quiet.

I wanted to make love not war, I wanted to pick flowers, I wanted to grow my hair long, I wanted peace, So I got up, and without thinking about it asked for a stage to sing on. Together with three friends, holding a guitar, despite feeling that my voice was shaking and that I was perspiring so much that my round glasses were covered in steam, so that I could hardly see who was sitting around me, and despite getting the words slightly muddled in my head ...something quite good came out..

All you need is love...

Everyone joined in with the chorus ...and I felt fine...

Now some of you are probably thinking: "Great, we get it, life is tough, we know that our lives are sometimes on the down side and our self confidence is sometimes beneath the floorboards, we know that sometimes all we want to do is to bang our heads on the wall, or pull the covers up over our heads and never go out...but want can we do about it? How can we make things better? How exactly is this book supposed to make us feel happy with ourselves?"

Imagine that you have discovered a secret key "The key to the power of thought" that will unlock the best way to:

-Control your thoughts like you control your muscles and change them from negative to positive.

-Change from being a pessimist to being an optimist simply by changing the way you talk.

-Get over your inferiority complexes.

-Most importantly – you will understand that what you think and feel affect the image you project to the outside and also affect your self confidence. Other people pick up on how you feel and treat you accordingly. In the end you attract into your life those things you thought about, whether they are good or bad!

This book, the second in the series, will help you learn those things that are really important in primary school that no class teacher tells you about. You will discover:

How to be positive think positive and feel positive.

Most importantly you'll learn how to be "simply me" and to survive primary school...

Back in the eighties I was in exactly the same situation that you are now...in primary school.

I didn't believe in myself, and had lots of negative thoughts about myself, and had to cope with all the difficulties that you are experiencing now. Until I decided that all this simply had to STOP!

In this book you'll find a lot of true stories about things that happened to me when I was your age...

And if I succeeded in getting through it all, anyone can!

So how will we do all of this?

As well as true stories, there are helpful tips and fun exercises, quizzes and questionnaires and your own personal journal which you can use to test exactly where you stand in different areas...

I recommend that you don't try to fool anyone when you read the book and fill in the questionnaires and your journal, especially not yourselves.

Answer the questions honestly-there are no wrong or right answers everything is right…

So …don't you want to start reading?

So, without waiting any more time, let's get started.

The Key to the Power of Thought

This Key helps us to understand how to control (or at least as far as possible) our thoughts, so that we start thinking positively instead of negatively.

The Key to 'The Power of Thought' helps us to understand that the things we think and feel not only affect our own self image and our self confidence, but they also affect the way that other people see us too. Our thoughts show on our faces and in the way we behave. Other people react to the way we are and treat us exactly as our own self image makes them see us. Our own thoughts and feelings dictate how other people relate to us, for better or for worse!

A True Story- A Positive Attitude

The hero of this story is none other than: a hand....yes, you got it right and you read it correctly- a hand!

When I was in fourth grade at school I made a very special friend, a girl who had just moved to the area where we lived. She was very pretty, smiled all the time, had sparkling blue eyes, was full of the joys of life and made friends with everyone very quickly because it was fun to spend time with her. Her name was Jane.

Jane had been born without a hand. Actually her right arm stopped at the elbow were she had two stumpy fingers with which she managed, believe it or not, to do everything: she wrote, she drew, she could scratch an itch, and could even peel tangerines.

When Jane first joined our class we could all see that she didn't have a hand but we soon forgot about it because she didn't make a big deal about it. She wore really cool clothes and wasn't embarrassed to wear sleeveless tops or T-shirts in the summer. She joined in with everything, she danced at parties and swam in the pool and did everything without feeling sorry for herself or trying to hide the fact that she only had one hand and without making out that she was in any way different to the rest of us.

And because Jane didn't make an issue of it, no one else did either.

My story starts on my birthday. It was the fashion in those days to have birthdays at sports centers in the gym. This gym was huge with all sorts of equipment including trampolines, vaulting boards, balance bars, hoops, ropes, climbing bars and lots more. The whole class arrived for the party and the sports coaches who were helping with the party divided us into small groups and the competitions started. Each group was supposed to complete as many exercises as possible on each set of equipment in the set time before moving on to the next piece of equipment. The winning team was the one who scored the most points over all.

Jane was in my group. When we came to the hoops which were suspended from the ceiling of the gym we were supposed to hang from them, holding on with both hands and swing backwards and forwards a few times.

When it was Jane's turn the coach said "You don't have to go up on the hoops, it doesn't matter." She gave him a cold, hard stared and her reply always gives me the goose bumps when I remember what she said: "I know that I only have one hand but that shouldn't make any difference. I would like you to help me up to the hoops and I'll manage to somehow to swing on them, you'll see."

The coach was stunned by Jane's determination and mental strength and said, "I see that you only have one hand, and I apologize for thinking that you can't swing on the hoops, I'm sure you'll be great." Having spoken, he lifted her up to the hoops. She held on to one hoop with her healthy hand and put her short arm through the second hoop. She managed to swing backwards and forwards and came down with a big grin on her face. Yes, Jane had managed to swing on the hoops even though she was missing a hand, just through her will power.

Do you want to hear the best part of my story about Jane?

We were having a real heart to heart discussion when I asked her "Jane, if you could have a hand now, what would you do?" She replied "What exactly do you think I'm supposed to do with a hand?"

Indeed, when her mother bought her a "gift" of a prosthetic hand- an artificial forearm and hand so she could look like everyone else, Jane took the plastic limb and threw it in the bin pointing at her elbow "This is my hand, and I'll decided just what I wear on top of it. Right now the only thing I am going to wear on it is a shirt..."

What can we learn from the story about Jane?

It all boils down to self confidence...

Even if you have some kind of problem, disability or difficulty if you believe in yourself and have self confidence you will go a long way.

If you make a big deal out of something that is bothering you, you can rest assured that other people will make a bigger deal out of it, and blow it up out of all proportion until it bothers them too. On the other hand if you don't feel sorry for yourself and don't behave as if it bothers you, then others will follow suit and will appreciate you and will stop paying attention to the problem and believe it or not...it will stop bothering you too.

The Rule for Perfection

We are all human, no-one is perfect. And you know what-so what!!! We can still feel good about who we are, and we can still like ourselves very much!

The Rule for the Power of Thought

If we think positively and believe in ourselves, then we behave accordingly and attract into our lives the things that we want. It works the other way too. If we have negative thoughts and our confidence is somewhere down beneath the floorboards then we behave in a way that ensures that's where we will end up.

A True Story Inferiority Complexes

When I was in fifth grade my school decided to start up a choir. This choir would meet to practice twice a week an hour before school started.

Everyone who wanted to join the choir had to audition for the music teacher and she sorted us into two groups, voice A and voice B.

I'm sure that you must be wondering who would be crazy enough to want to come into school an hour early for choir practice.

However, it turned out that choir was the most popular club of all and every single member of the class turned up for the auditions.

We knew that the choir members would miss quite a few lessons rehearsing for special concerts and that the choir would sing at all the special occasions at school and at other places too, like hospitals and old people's homes.

The teacher played a song on the piano and the pupils took it in turn to sing with her.

Then the teacher determined the pupil's fate: Voice A (for the high voices) or voice B (for the low voices).

It turned out that everyone passed their auditions and we were all sorted into voice A or voice B, with all the girls being voice A and all the boys...and Orly being voice B. I was the only girl who was supposed to sing voice B!

I often used to have sore throats and get a little hoarse, but to be told straight out that I had a boy's voice was another story all together.

I was the odd one out. I didn't want to be the only girl singing with the boys. I didn't know whether to quit the choir or whether to keep on going???

This isn't the end of the story. I carried on going to choir practice.

We were rehearsing for the Christmas concert which we would sing at the following month. We turned up at the crack of dawn. We were practicing singing a medley of carols in two voices... 'Silent Night' , 'O come all ye faithful', 'Away in a manger" and all sorts of other carols. Then, the day before the concert IT happened.

We were in the middle of 'Silent Night' (I was only singing la la la as voice B was only singing the background voices, or should I say background noises, while voice A was singing all of the words), when I suddenly felt that the teacher had fixed her eyes on me with a piercing glare and without take her eyes off me was heading straight towards me. She then said the following words which became engraved on my heart in a loud voice which everyone could hear. The teacher said:

"Orly, can't you hear that you're singing out of tune? In the concert tomorrow I want you just to move your lips without singing."

Excuse me...had I heard right? I couldn't believe that this was happening to me. I had never thought there was a problem with my voice, but I did now.

Needless to say I left the choir (only after I had stood on stage just moving my lips throughout the entire

Christmas carol concert...) and I started to develop a serious inferiority complex about my voice. I stopped singing out loud in public all together. Whenever there was a school assembly or any other reason to sing together I only moved my lips...

After a while my mother shared a story about a complex she herself had experienced.

When she had been a small baby she had fallen out of her pram, had cracked her skull open and had, ever since then, lived with a scar across the centre of her forehead.

Her mother (my grandmother) had told her that she should always keep her scar hidden by wearing her hair with long bangs.

My mother dutifully always had heavy bangs which completely covered her scar. Whenever any of the hair's in her bangs moved ever so slightly my mother was careful to put them back in place straight away.

When my mother met my father he suggested that a different shorter hairstyle without bangs may suit her better. My mother refused to listen and when my father asked why she insisted on having bangs my mother looked him straight in the eye, parted her bangs and said "Because of this"…

"Because of what?" my father asked, not understanding what she was trying to hint at. "Because of this" My mother replied, pointing to the scar on her forehead.

My father still had no idea of what she was talking about, until she explained the whole story to him. He replied that she had all the proof she needed today to realize that the whole thing was in her head. The only person who could see the scar was my mother herself.

My mother was finally convinced, parted with her fringe and forgot about her scar.

Then my mother turned to me, looked me in the eye and said, "Orly this inferiority complex is all in your head. No one pays any attention at all to whether or not you can sing, except for you yourself.

If you stop worrying about it you'll see that it stops being important.

I decided to accept what my mother had to say, and while I'm never going to be a famous opera singer, there's nothing wrong with singing in the shower and I enjoy singing from time to time.

I've stopped letting my inferiority complex control me! How about you?

The Rule for Inferiority Complexes

We keep our inferiority complexes deep inside of our heads and in our thoughts. If we focus too much attention on them those around us see them too...and if we don't pay them any attention, then no one notices them.

Do you suffer from an inferiority complex?

Circle the answer which best fits how you would behave in each one of the following situations.

	Of course not	Probably not	Maybe	Probably	Definitely
Your parents don't speak English well and have strong accents. Would you be ashamed to bring friends home?	1	2	3	4	5
You woke up in the morning, looked in the mirror and could no longer see your face, only an enormous spot which had grown over night on the tip of your nose and made your nose at least half a centimeter longer. Would you decide	1	2	3	4	5

to stay home in bed under the covers so no one sees the 'growth'.					
You walk past a really good looking group of boys / girls. Would you stare at the ground as you go past so they won't notice you.	1	2	3	4	5
Your teacher has called your name and has asked you to come and stand in front of the class to answer a question. Would you stare at the ground and speak in a very quiet voice?	1	2	3	4	5
Your friends are all extremely well off. Their parents live in spacious houses and drive expensive	1	2	3	4	5

cars. They wear expensive fashion labels and eat out in posh restaurants. Your house is far more ordinary than those your friends live in. Would you try to keep that a secret and not invite them to your house?					

The analysis
Add up your scores and see where you fit

5-11
You don't have inferiority complexes. You're happy with yourself just the way you are, and don't care what anyone else may say. Even if you're having a bad hair day you don't feel you have to cover it up under a scarf or cap-good for you, keep it up!

12-18
On the one hand you are happy with who you are, but there are things you are not completely confident about or happy with the way they are. That's fine, no

one is superman and perfection is for Barbie dolls.

19-25

You do have inferiority complexes-big time! If you could you would stay at home all day long under the bedcovers so that no one could see you. This is my advice. Almost everyone has some kind of inferiority complex, you're not alone. As soon as you really understand and accept that it's not only you who suffers from acne and gets enormous spots on the end of your nose...you'll be able to find the courage to face the world. We're all human and no-one is perfect. And who cares??? We don't have to be perfect to feel good about ourselves. Think about it...

A True Story Birthday Tears

We had a special custom in our class at school. We used to celebrate everyone's birthday first thing in the morning in school before lessons began. We had a class committee which collected money from everyone in the class a few days before the birthday to buy presents and on the morning of the birthday we would celebrate with balloons and decorate the classroom, write all sorts of greetings on the board, sing songs and make a big fuss of the birthday boy or girl.

Rob was my next door neighbor and was in the same class as me at school. We used to go to school together and come back home together too. This story took place when I was ill and had been off school for a few days.

Rob told me all about it after it happened.

The morning of the February the 3rd was a special morning. It was Rob's birthday. He had felt excited from the moment he got up looking forward to his celebration in the classroom.

He imagined what it would be like walking into the classroom especially decorated, just for him, with everyone jumping up to 'surprise' him and wish him with 'Happy Birthday!' and singing songs. He imagined the colors of all the shiny balloons he'd be given. He tried to guess what greeting each of his classmates would have written on the board. He arrived at the door to the classroom and something seemed wrong. He couldn't hear anything unusual. He opened the door and saw...nothing! The classroom was exactly the same as it had been yesterday and the day before.

There wasn't a single balloon anywhere in sight. There were no greetings on the perfectly clean blackboard. No-one was singing and no-one leapt up to wish him 'Happy Birthday'. There was nothing!

Rob was shocked. He had been so excited but now he was even more hurt and offended. Why had he been left out? Why of everyone in the class had they decided to ignore his birthday?

Rob had been in a terrible mood for all of the rest of the day. He didn't tell anyone how upset he was, he just was annoyed and angry and quarreled with everyone.

He came to visit me on his way home, to bring me the homework. I could see from his expression that something was wrong.

He seemed sad, on the verge of tears.

"What happened Rob?"

He gave me a furious look and stared me straight in the eyes

"You too??? You've forgotten that it's my birthday today as well?"

"How was I supposed to know? I've been off school for almost a week. I didn't hear any of the preparations that the birthday committee made."

"That's just it" Rob replied. "They didn't make any. Those selfish pigs didn't do a single thing for my birthday. There weren't any balloons, no one had bought presents, there weren't any greetings on the board, no one even wished me 'Happy Birthday'. They didn't do anything. I never want to speak to them again! I'm through with them. I am never ever going to celebrate another birthday at school. They can all vanish into thin air as far as I'm concerned."

"Rob, did you talk to them beforehand?" I asked. "Are you sure they knew it was your birthday?"

"Of course they knew" he answered. "They've got a list of all the dates and they ignored mine on purpose. You've got no idea how it feels when you're the only one to be missed out, and not have their birthday celebrated. It's never happened to you."

I felt sorry for him, and was very puzzled. Rob had lots of friends and everyone liked him. They couldn't have decided to ignore his birthday on purpose.

I went back to school the next day and straight away spoke to the 'birthday committee' to try and find out what had gone wrong.

"You mean to say it was Rob's birthday yesterday?" they exclaimed in amazement.

"Yes, and you didn't do anything for him. Do you know how it feels to be completely ignored by everyone on your birthday? It won't happen to you because you're on the committee."

Simon got out the list of names of all the class members with the dates of their birthdays next to each name. "Let's have a look at the list" he suggested. "We can't have just forgotten to check."

Simon spread the list on his desk. We all looked and next to Rob's name the date was penciled in as 3/2 meaning the second of March not the third of February.

What can we learn from this story?

Rob was being pessimistic. He was certain that everyone had ignored him on purpose. He got into a horrible mood, wallowed in his own self pity, felt miserable and was upset with everyone and didn't think for one minute that there may be a different simple explanation to what had happened.

If he had taken a different approach and hadn't let himself get angry so quickly and had been thinking along positive optimistic lines of thought then he could have gone to the birthday committee and talked things over with them. He would have found out straight away that they'd simply made a mistake...a human error.

Rob would have spared himself a whole lot of crying, anger and upset. They could have celebrated his birthday the very next day.

That's the difference between optimists and pessimists.

We can actually practice thinking differently. We can train ourselves to look on the bright side and think positively instead of thinking negatively. Try it, it's worthwhile!

The Rule for Pessimists

Pessimists always look at the dark side of things, and the half empty cup. They think negative thoughts, think the worst will happen, feel sorry for themselves and think that they have the worst possible deal with bad things always happening just to them.

The Rule for Optimists

Optimists look to the bright side of life. They see the half full cup and think positive thoughts, and believe in themselves and in their abilities. If something bad happens to them they believe that it happened by chance by accident, and believe that tomorrow things will be better...

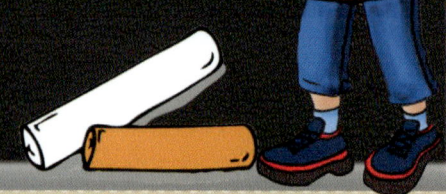

SimplyMe

Writing about Myself- Worksheets:
The Key to the Power of Thought

1. Thinking positively creates positive outcomes…and vice versa…

Have you ever thought that something good was going to happen, and behaved like it really would happen and then it did?

1. What did you think about?

_____
_____
_____

2. What did you do about it?

_____
_____
_____

3. What actually happened?

_____
_____
_____

The opposite scenario... have you ever been worried that something bad might happen, and behaved like it really would happen and then it did?

1. What did you think about?
   _____
   _____
   _____

2. What did you do about it?
   _____
   _____
   _____

3. What actually happened?
   _____
   _____
   _____

2. Close Surveillance:

In the same way that people who want to lose weight count calories, people can keep a close watch over their negative voices (that whisper in our ear's that we won't succeed...that we're not good enough...) and by keeping watch on them lessen their activities.

1. Which three negative voices (negative thoughts) are most active in your head?

_____
_____
_____

2. What do they whisper to you?

_____
_____
_____

3. When do they 'attack'?

_____
_____
_____

The name of the negative voice:	
What it says:	
When it attacks:	

The name of the negative voice:	
What it says:	
When it attacks:	

The name of the negative voice:	
What it says:	
When it attacks:	

3. Optimism versus Pessimism:

Are you optimistic or pessimistic?

1. Check the language you use. Write down the types of sentences you use. Are they optimistic (I know that I'll succeed, of course everything will be OK) or pessimistic (I never succeed, I never get a chance).

2. If you use pessimistic sentences change them into optimistic ones, and see what happens after you say them.

A pessimistic sentence.	The pessimistic sentence turned into an optimistic sentence.

We can't finish without a short summary...

Dear friends,

We've come to the end of this part of our journey towards 'discovering myself'. I wanted to thank you for coming along for the ride, so together we could make some important discoveries on that important question 'how can we survive primary school?'

This book is the second in the series of books which together can help you learn those things that are really important to know in primary school and practice them until they become second nature. It explains things that you've always wondered about, and wanted to know, but class teachers just don't explain.

This book has introduced you to 'the key to the power of thought' which has let you into the following secrets:

- -How to control your thoughts like you control your muscles and change them from negative to positive.

- -How to change from being a pessimist to being an optimist simply by changing the way you talk.

- How to get over your inferiority complexes.

- Most importantly – you have understood that what you think and feel affects the image you project to the outside and also affects your self confidence. You know that other people pick up on how you feel and treat you accordingly. You have learnt how to attract those things you want into your life.

Now its time to get to work and start practicing to 'Be positive, think positive and feel positive!'

By using this key which is so, so simple you can feel happy, contented, satisfied, charming, beautiful, rich, wonderful, clever, cool, popular, loved, amazing,

admired, hypnotizing, awesome, astounding, brilliant, cute, charismatic, hot, wicked, cool dudes, positive, friendly, sought after, sexy and everything else....

Seriously now:

Using this Key will help you to simply be you...who you really are and to feel good about yourselves and with what you want and with the things you do.

All I have left to say is that I hope you enjoyed reading this as much as I enjoyed writing it.

Now…it's time to get busy… so .get started putting everything you have learnt into practice!

Wishing you all things good,

orly

Thank you for purchasing this book!

It is very important to me to get your feedback and hear what you think!

Please write a review on Amazon and let me know your thoughts.

Other Books by Dr. Orly Katz:

peer pressure vs. true friends!
Surviving Primary School Vol. 1

Be Positive! Think Positive! Feel Positive!
Surviving Primary School Vol. 2

Body Language, Intution & Leadership!
Surviving Primary School Vol. 3

Passions, Strengths and Self Esteem-
The Extensive Guide!
Surviving Primary School Vol. 4

Other Books by Dr. Orly Katz:

peer pressure vs. true friends!
Surviving Junior High Vol. 1

Be Positive! Think Positive! Feel Positive!
Surviving Junior High Vol. 2

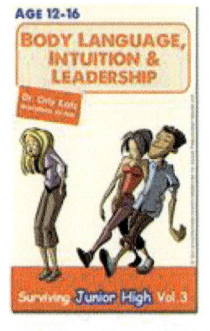

Body Language, Intution & Leadership!
Surviving Junior High Vol. 3

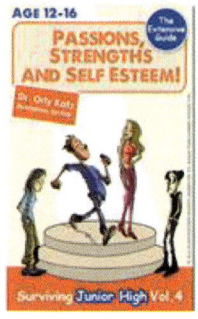

Passions, Strengths and Self Esteem-
The Extensive Guide!
Surviving Junior High Vol. 4

Printed in Great Britain
by Amazon